Alexander Girard
COLOR

AMMO

this book is dedicated in memory of

Alexander Girard

1907-1993

there
are
so
many
colors,
everywhere
you
look;

alexander girard, shows us colors in this book.

girls
wearing
blue,

green,
and
purple;

a long, black snake, curled up in a circle.

a green,
four leaf
clover,
that's very
lucky too;

pink, white, and green eyes, all watching you!

a pretty,
patterned
palace,
in
black
and
white;

orange, pink, and yellow stripes, all very bright.

a mother
and
child,
with
eyes
of blue;

pretty, pink flowers, just for you.

a bright,
red-orange
sun,
that loves
to sing;

a
lonely,
little
angel,
with
light
blue
wings.

red, green, and blue stripes, orange stripes and more;

a few
black
birds;
i think
there
are
four?

a
daisy
in
the
garden,
green
and
growing;

multi-colored friends, where are they going?

**lots
of
shapes,
in a
big,
red
sun;**

a colorful painting, because painting is fun.

**bright,
red suns,
all with
smiling
faces;**

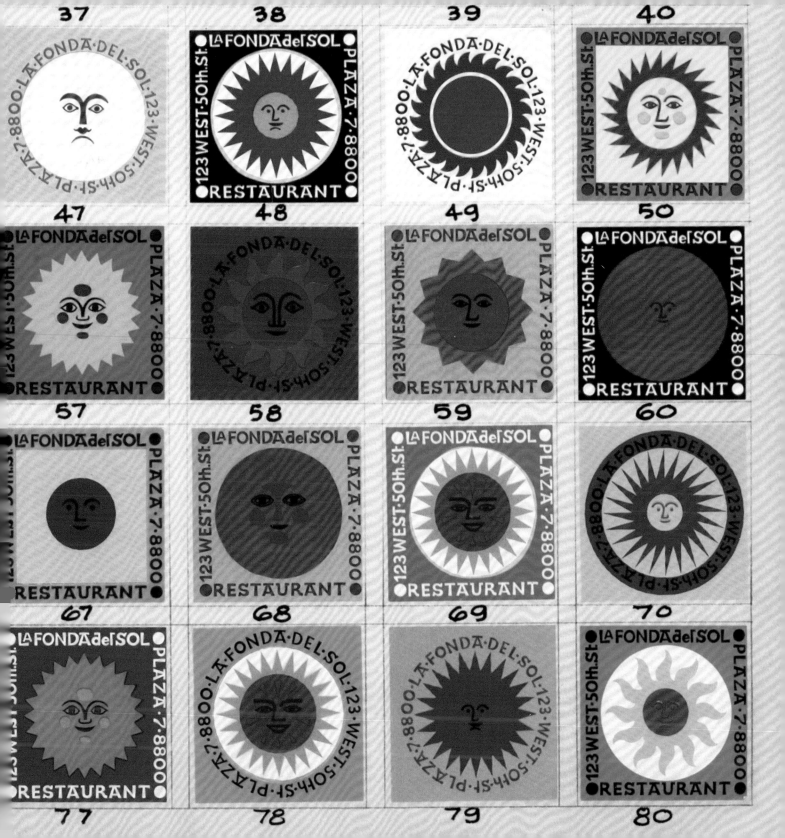

black
and
white
friends,
going
lots
of
places.

a big,
round
moon,
in
blue
and
black;

**black
on
white
letters,
all in
a stack.**

FSPBJ8NC&
Q1WAH4EIZ
KUY67DX9G
3MOT2V5LR
FSPBJ8NC&
Q1WAH4EIZ
KUY67DX9G
3MOT2V5LR
FSPBJ8NC&

a
bouquet
of
red
flowers,
for
my
love;

a
branch
of a
tree,
and a
pretty
white
dove.

a
multi-
colored
village,
where
there's
lots to
do;

a big,
red
heart,
just
to say
i love
you.

© 2011 AMMO Books, LLC | All rights reserved
Printed in China
ISBN: 978-162326004-0

Designed and written by: Gloria Fowler
Girard Fonts: House Industries

Special thanks to:
Kori Girard and the entire Girard Family
Todd Oldham
Steve, Miles, and Lola Crist

For more children's books and products visit us at:
www.ammobooks.com